POP
SONGS FOR
The Wedding

ISBN 1-57560-378-0

Copyright © 2000 Cherry Lane Music Company
International Copyright Secured   All Rights Reserved

Visit our website at www.cherrylane.com

Wedding Memories

Date/Time

_____

Ceremony Location

_____

_____

Bride

_____

Groom

_____

Officiated By

_____

Maid Of Honor

_____

Best Man

_____

Bridesmaids

_____

_____

_____

_____

_____

Ushers

_____

_____

_____

_____

_____

 # Music Planner

• CEREMONY MOMENT •

Performance Time		Selections
Prelude	_____	_____
First Solo	_____	_____
Second Solo	_____	_____
Processional	_____	_____
Recessional	_____	_____
Postlude	_____	_____

• RECEPTION MUSIC •

Reception Activity	Time	General Kind of Music/Selections
Receiving Line	_____	_____
Arrival of Bride and Groom	_____	_____
First Dance	_____	_____
Father and Bride Dance	_____	_____
Mother and Groom Dance	_____	_____
Cake Cutting	_____	_____
Dancing or Background	_____	_____
Special Requests	_____	_____

• PERFORMERS •

Organist (or Main Instrumentalist) _____

Soloist _____

Ensemble or Choir Leader _____

Ensemble Members _____

_____

Almost Paradise
Love Theme from the Paramount Motion Picture FOOTLOOSE

Words by
Dean Pitchford

Music by
Eric Carmen

Amazed

Moderately slow Country Ballad

Words and Music by
Chris Lindsey, Marv Green
and Aimee Mayo

Ev - 'ry time our eyes meet, this feel - in' in - side me
The smell of your skin, the taste of your kiss,

is al - most more_ than I_ can take._
the way you whis - per in_ the dark._

*Recorded a half step lower.

I don't know how you do what you do.___ I'm so in love_ with you._

___ It just keeps get-tin' bet - ter.

I wan-na spend the rest of my life___ with you by my side___ for-ev-er and ev-

er.

Ev-'ry lit-tle thing that you do,___

1. G   A

ba-by, I'm a - mazed by you.

2. G   A   C   D

ba-by, I'm a - mazed by you.

A   C   G   Dsus4   D   G

Ev-'ry lit - tle thing that you do.

A   Bm   G

I'm so in love with you.   It just keeps get-tin' bet - ter.

Can't Help Falling in Love

Words and Music by
George David Weiss, Hugo Peretti
and Luigi Creatore

13

Annie's Song

Words and Music by
John Denver

rain, _____ Like a storm in the des -

ert, _____ like a sleep - y blue o - cean, _____

_____ You fill up my sen - ses, _____ come

fill me a - gain. _____ Come let me

Beautiful in My Eyes

Words and Music by
Joshua Kadison

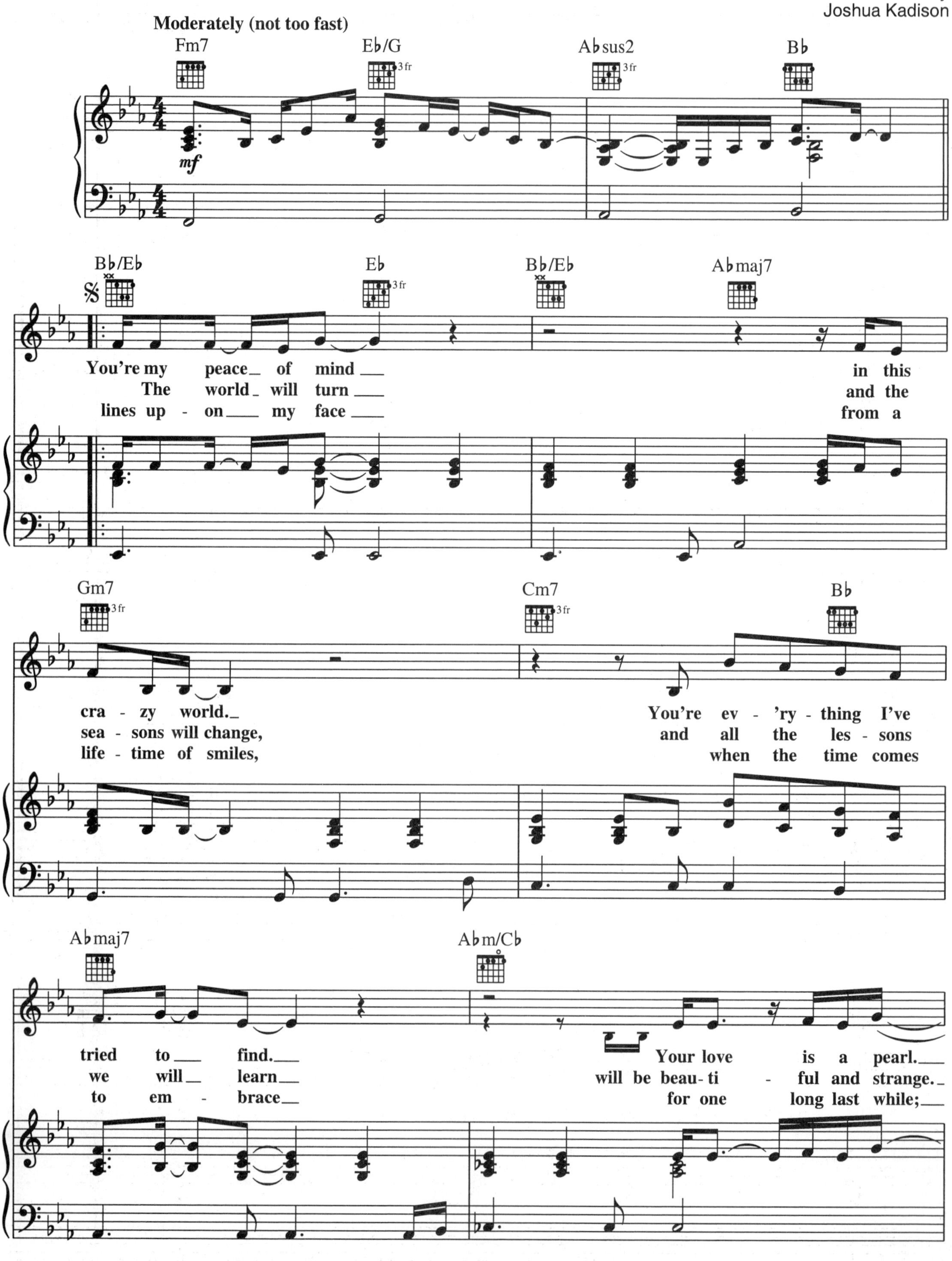
Moderately (not too fast)
Fm7
Eb/G
Absus2
Bb
mf
Bb/Eb
Eb
Bb/Eb
Abmaj7
You're my peace_ of mind ___ in this
The world_ will turn ___ and the
lines up - on ___ my face ___ from a
Gm7
Cm7
Bb
cra - zy world._ You're ev - 'ry - thing I've
sea - sons will change, and all the les - sons
life - time of smiles, when the time comes
Abmaj7
Abm/Cb
tried to ___ find.___ Your love is a pearl.___
we will_ learn___ will be beau - ti - ful and strange._
to em - brace___ for one long last while;___

23

Could I Have This Dance

from URBAN COWBOY

Words and Music by
Wayland Holyfield and Bob House

I'll always re-mem-ber the song they were
al-ways re-mem-ber that mag-ic

play-ing the first time _____ we danced and I knew.
mo-ment, when I held _____ you close to me.

As we swayed to the mu-sic _____ and held to each
As we moved to-geth-er, _____ I knew for -

oth - er, _____ I fell in love with __ you.
ev - er _____ you're all I'll ev - er _____ need.

Could I have this dance for the rest of my

life? Would you be my part - ner _____ ev - 'ry

night? When we're to - geth - er, it feels __ so

Follow Me

Words and Music by
John Denver

*Guitarists: Tune lowest string to D.

me.

A

A7

Fol-low me ___ up and down,

G/E

D

G

all ___ the way and all a - round,

D

G   A7   D

Take my hand ___ and say you'll fol-low me.

A

It's long been on my mind, ___ you know it's
You see, I'd like to share my life with you and

mp

G

D

Bm

been a long, long time, I'll try to find the
show you things ___ I've seen, places that I'm

way that I can make you un- der- stand _____ The
going to _____ places where_ I've been _____ to

way I feel a- bout_____ you and just how much I need you_____ To be
have you there be- side_____ me and nev - er be a - lone and

there where I can talk to you when there's no one else a - round._
all the time can that you're with me, then we will be at home._

After repeat, **D.S.** 𝄋 *al* ⊕ *Coda*

Coda

way._____

Take my hand_ and say you'll fol - low me.

29

Dance Little Bird
(The Chicken Dance)

By Terry Rendall and Werner Thomas

Don't Know Much

Words and Music by
Barry Mann, Cynthia Weil
and Tom Snow

that may be _____ all I need _ to know.   Look at these eyes,

they've nev - er   seen what mat - ters. ___   Look at these dreams, __

so beat - en ___   and so bat - tered. _____   I don't know ___ much,

but I know I   love you, _____   and

that may be _____ all I, I need to know.

So man-y ques-tions still left un-an-swered.

So much I've nev-er bro-ken through. ___

But when I feel you near me some-times I see so clear-ly.

that may be _____ all I need _ to know.

I don't know _ much, but I know I love you, _____

and that may be _____ all there is to

know. _____ Woh. _____

Endless Love

from ENDLESS LOVE

Words and Music by
Lionel Richie

For Baby

(For Bobbie)

Words and Music by
John Denver

For You

Words and Music by
John Denver

Just to long for your kiss - es, _____ just to dream of your
Just a rea - son for liv - ing, _____ just to say I a -

sighs, just to know that I'd give my life for
dore, just to know that you're here in my heart to

you.
stay. } _cresc._ For you, all the rest _____
_____ of my life. _____ For you, all the best _____ of my life. _____ For

you a - lone, _____ on - ly for you. Just to wake up each

_mf_

dim.

Give Me Forever

(I Do)

Words and Music by
Carter Cathcart, John Tesh,
Juni Morrison and James Ingram

Looking out,___ I see,___ and I

With this ring___ I'm bound,___ and I

To love you, I love you, I

To love you, I love you, I do.

Glory of Love
Theme from KARATE KID PART II

Words and Music by
David Foster, Peter Cetera
and Diane Nini

Lyrics:
To - night__ it's ver - y clear, as we're both stand - ing here,__ there's__ so man - y things I want____ to say.__

We'll live for-ev - er, know-ing to-geth - er that we

did it all for the glo - ry of love. ___

Just like a knight in shin-ing ar - mor, from a long time a-go,

just in time I will save the day, ___ take you to my cas - tle far a - way. ___

I am the man who will fight for your hon - or,

I'll be the he - ro that you're ___ dream - ing of. ___ We're

gon-na live for-ev-er, know-ing to-geth-er that we

did it all___ for the glo-ry of love.___

We'll live for-ev-er, know-ing to-geth-er that we

Here, There and Everywhere

Words and Music by
John Lennon and Paul McCartney

I Love You

from the Paramount Motion Picture RUNAWAY BRIDE

Words and Music by
Tammy Hyler, Keith Follese
and Adrienne Follese

The sun is shin-in'
I nev-er knew that I could

ev-'ry day, clouds nev-er get in the way for you and me. ___
feel like this, can hard-ly wait till our next kiss. You're so cool. ___

I've known you just a
If I'm dream-in', please don't

I Want to Know What Love Is

Words and Music by
Mick Jones

I've got-ta take a lit-tle time,

a lit-tle time to think things o-ver.

I bet-ter read be-tween the lines,____ in case I

need it when__ I'm old ____ er.____

Now, this moun-tain I____ must climb____ feels like the world up - on____ my shoul -
I'm gon-na take a lit-tle time,____ a lit-tle time to look__ a-round____

change this lone - ly life._____ I want to know what love is.___

_____ I want you to show___ me.

I want to feel what love is.___ I know you can show___ me.___

_____ me.

D.S. and fade

75

If

Words and Music by
David Gates

Just the Two of Us

Words and Music by
Ralph MacDonald, William Salter
and Bill Withers

cas-tles in— the sky.— Just the two of us, you and I.—

Just the Way You Are

Words and Music by
Billy Joel

I need to know ___ that you ___ will al - ways be ___ the same old some - one that I knew. ___ Oh, what will ___ it take ___ till you ___ be - lieve _____ in me ___ the way that I _____ be - lieve ___ in you? ___

Longer

Words and Music by
Dan Fogelberg

CODA

I'll be in love __ with you. __

Long-er than __ there've been

Love Me Tender

Words and Music by
Elvis Presley and Vera Matson

A Love Until the End of Time

Words by Carol Connors

Music by Lee Holdridge

May You Always

Words and Music by
Larry Markes and Dick Charles

My Sweet Lady

Words and Music by
John Denver

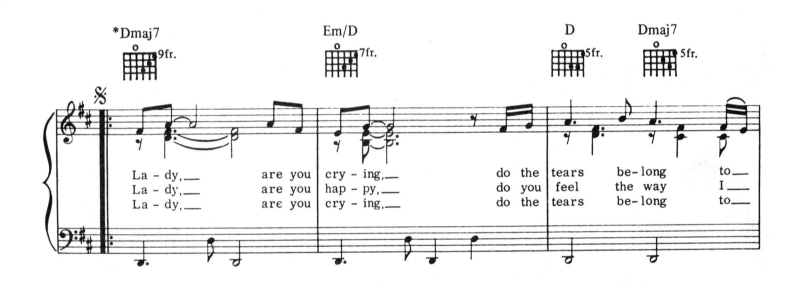

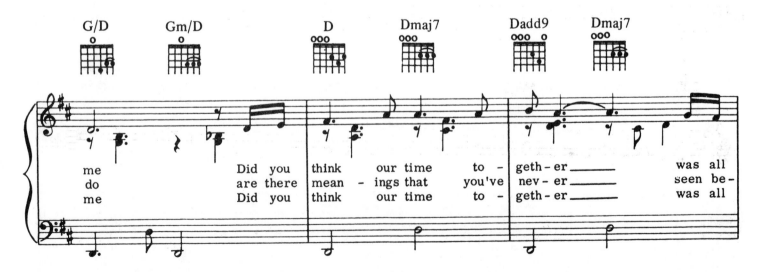

*Guitarists: Tune lowest string to D.

Sometimes When We Touch

Words by Dan Hill

Music by Barry Mann

both break down _____ and cry. _____ I wan‑na

hold you till the fear _____ in me _____ sub‑

To Coda ⊕

1. sides.

Ro‑ sides.

At

cresc.

times I'd like___ to break___ you and drive___ you to___ your knees.___

At times I'd like___ to break___ through___ and

hold___ you end - less - ly.___ At

sides.___

Perhaps Love

Words and Music by
John Denver

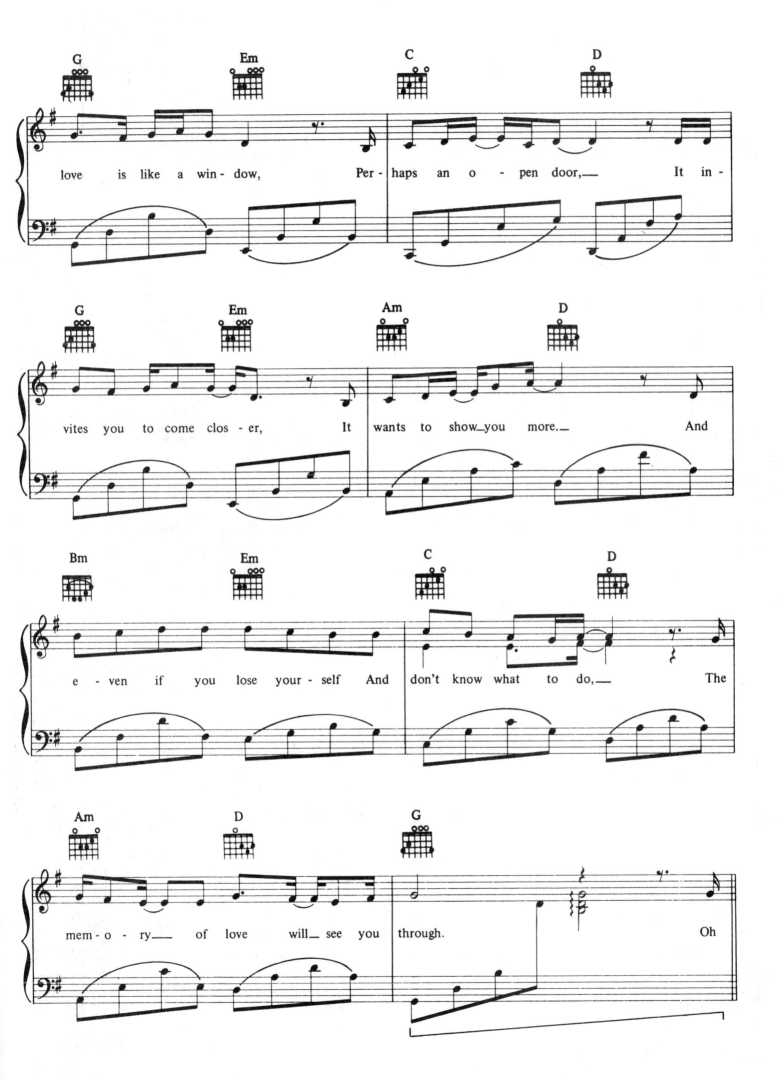

love is like the o - cean, Full of con - flict, full of change, Like a

in tempo

fire___ when it's cold___ out - side,___ Or thun - der when it rains.___ If

I should live for - ev - er And all my dreams come true, My

mem - o - ries ___ of love will___ be of you.

slowing

Save the Best for Last

Words and Music by
Phil Galdston, Jon Lind
and Wendy Waldman

To Coda ⊕

I see the pas - sion in _____ your eyes. _____
You won - dered how _____ you'd make _____ it through. _____
Just when I thought _____ a chance _____ had passed, _____

Some - times it's all _____ a big _____ sur - prise. _____
I won - dered what _____ was wrong _____ with you. _____
you go and save _____ the best _____ for last. _____

'Cause there was a time _____ when all _____ I did _____
'Cause how could you give _____ your love _____ to some -

_____ was wish _____ you'd tell _____ me this _____ was love. _____
- one else _____ and share _____ your dreams _____ with me? _____

117

It's not the way ____ I hoped ____ or ____ how ____
Some - times the ver - y thing ____ you're ____ look -

I planned, ____ but some - how it's e - nough. ____
- ing for ____ is the one thing it's you can't see. ____

And now we're stand - ing face ____ to face. ____
But now we're stand - ing face ____ to face. ____

Is - n't this world ____ a cra - zy place? ____

Just when I thought _____ our chance___ had passed,_

_ you go and save _____ the best ___ for last. _

All of the nights___

Someone Like You

from JEKYLL & HYDE

Words by Leslie Bricusse

Music by Frank Wildhorn

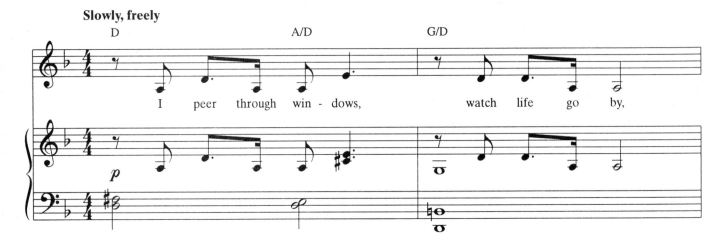

I peer through win-dows, watch life go by, dream of to-mor-row, and won-der "why?"

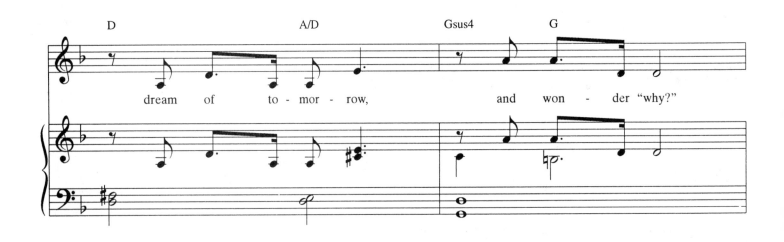

The past is hold-ing me, keep-ing life at bay.

ev - er be the same! There'd be a new way to live____ a

new life to love,____ if some - one like you____ found

me! Oh, if some - one____ like you found

some - one____ like me, then sud - den - ly____ noth - ing would

Take Me as I Am

from JEKYLL & HYDE

Words by Leslie Bricusse

Music by Frank Wildhorn

Moderately slow

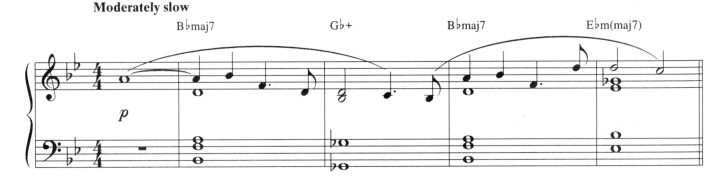

Jekyll: Some-times I see past the ho-ri- zon,
Emma: Look in my eyes, who do you see there?

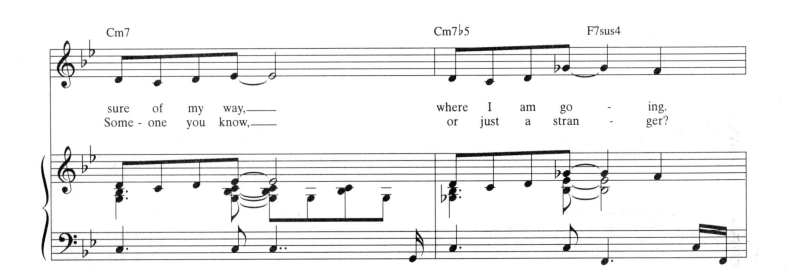

sure of my way, where I am go- ing.
Some-one you know, or just a stran- ger?

But where's the prize_____ I have my eyes_____ on?
If you are wise,_____ you will see me_____ there!

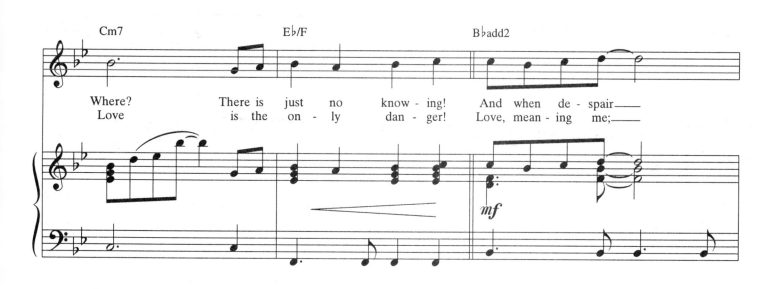

Where? There is just no know - ing! And when de - spair_____
Love is the on - ly dan - ger! Love, mean - ing me;_____

tears me in two,_____ who can I turn_____ to but you?_____
love, mean - ing you._____ We'll make that one_____ dream come true!_____

Through the Years

Words and Music by
Steve Dorff and Marty Panzer

Till I Loved You

from GOYA

Music and Lyrics by
Maury Yeston

cer - tain _____ mo - ment _____ when I loved _____

you! No joy ev - er en - tered my

room when my room was with - out you. _____ My

love nev - er came in - to bloom till each thought was a - bout you. _____

142

Tonight I Celebrate My Love

Words and Music by
Michael Masser and Gerry Goffin

(I've Had)
The Time of My Life
from DIRTY DANCING

Words and Music by
Franke Previte, John DeNicola
and Donald Markowitz

owe it all to you. _____

Male: I've been wait-ing for so long; _____ now I've

fi-n'lly found some-one _ to stand by me. _____ *Female:* We saw the

writ - ing on the wall _____ as we felt this mag - i - cal __ fan - ta -

sy. _____

Both: Now with

pas - sion in our eyes _____ there's no way we could dis - guise _____ it se - cret -

ly. _____

So we

take each oth-er's hand _____ 'cause we seem to un - der - stand _____ the ur - gen -

148

some - thing: ___ *Both:* this could be love. Be - cause I've ___ had ___
I've

___ the time of my life. ___ No, I nev - er felt ___ this way be -
had the time of my life. ___ And I've searched through ev - 'ry o - pen

fore. Yes, I swear it's the truth, _____ and I
door till I've found the ___ truth, _____ and I

owe it all to you. ___ 'Cause owe it all to you. _____

Unchained Melody

featured in the Motion Picture GHOST

Lyric by
Hy Zaret

Music by
Alex North

Oh, my love, my dar - ling, I've hun - gered for your touch a long, lone - ly time. _____ Time goes by so slow - ly and time can do so

much, are you still mine? _____ I

need your love, _____ I need your love, _____ God

speed your love _____ to me! _____

Lone - ly riv - ers flow _____ to the sea, _____ to the
Lone - ly moun - tains gaze _____ at the stars, _____ at the

poco rall.

a tempo

poco rall.

a tempo

poco accel.

R.H.

L.H.

R.H.

L.H.

You Decorated My Life

Words and Music by
Debbie Hupp and Bob Morrison

All my life was a pa - per _ once plain, pure and white; _
rhyme with no rea - son _ in an un - fin - ished song; _

Till you moved with your pen _ chang - in' moods now and then _ till the
There was no har - mo - ny _ life meant noth - in' to me, _ un - til

bal - ance was right. _ Then you add - ed some mu - sic, _
you came a - long. _ And you brought out the col - ors, _

Waiting for a Girl Like You

Words and Music by
Mick Jones and Lou Gramm

Wedding March

(Bridal Chorus)
from the opera LOHENGRIN

By Richard Wagner

When I Fall in Love

featured in the TriStar Motion Picture SLEEPLESS IN SEATTLE

Words by
Edward Heyman

Music by
Victor Young

Slowly, with much feeling

cool in the warmth of the sun. When I give my heart it will be com-

plete-ly, or I'll nev-er give my heart; _____ And the

mo-ment I can feel that you feel that way too is when I fall in

love with you. _____ you. _____

You Needed Me

Words and Music by
Randy Goodrum

Moderately